Y O U R

TRUE
REFLECTION

STUDY GUIDE

For foreign and subsidiary rights, contact the author.

Cover design: Cover design by: Sara Young

ISBN: 978-1-959095-38-5   1 2 3 4 5 6 7 8 9 10

Printed in the United States of America

YOUR
TRUE
REFLECTION

TRADE IN WHAT YOU SEE
FOR WHAT GOD SEES

DON ANKENBRANDT

STUDY GUIDE

CONTENTS

Chapter 1. You Are Adopted 6

Chapter 2. You Have Access to the Father 8

Chapter 3. You Are Alive.. 10

Chapter 4. You Are Appointed to Serve 12

Chapter 5. You Are Blameless.................................. 14

Chapter 6. You Are Blessed.................................... 16

Chapter 7. You Are Brought Near............................. 18

Chapter 8. You Are Built 20

Chapter 9. You Are Buried with Christ 22

Chapter 10. You Are Chosen 24

Chapter 11. You Are a Child of God........................... 26

Chapter 12. You Are a Citizen 28

Chapter 13. You Are Content in Your Sufficiency 30

Chapter 14. You Wear the Crown of Life..................... 32

Chapter 15. You Are Crucified with Christ 34

Chapter 16. You Are Debt Free 36

Chapter 17. You Are Delivered and Transferred 38

Chapter 18. You Are Entrusted with the Gospel.............. 40

Chapter 19. You Have Eternal Life............................. 42

Chapter 20. You Are Fearless 44

Chapter 21. You Are Forgiven 46

Chapter 22. You Are Free....................................... 48

Chapter 23. You Are Gifted 50

Chapter 24. You Have Grace 52

Chapter 25. You Are Heard 54

Chapter 26. You Are the Heir of All Things 56

Chapter 27. You Are Hidden in Christ......................... 58

Chapter 28. You Are Holy and Made Complete................ 60

Chapter 29. You Are a Lavished Child of God 62

Chapter 30. You Are the Light of the World.................. 64

Chapter 31. You Are Loved... 66

Chapter 32. You Have Mercy... 68

Chapter 33. You Are More than a Conqueror...................... 70

Chapter 34. You Are a New Creation................................... 72

Chapter 35. You Have a New Name 74

Chapter 36. You Are No Longer Condemned 76

Chapter 37. You Are No Longer in Need 78

Chapter 38. You Are an Overcomer 80

Chapter 39. You Are Overflowing with Hope...................... 82

Chapter 40. You Are a Partaker 84

Chapter 41. You Have Peace 86

Chapter 42. You Have Power... 88

Chapter 43. You Are Predestined 90

Chapter 44. You Have Precious and Great Promises........... 92

Chapter 45. You Are Raised with Christ 94

Chapter 46. You Are Reconciled.. 96

Chapter 47. You Are Redeemed 98

Chapter 48. You Are Restored 100

Chapter 49. You Have Rewards in Heaven that Await You 102

Chapter 50. You Are Rich in Inheritance 104

Chapter 51. You Are Righteous 106

Chapter 52. You Are a Royal Priesthood........................... 108

Chapter 53. You Are a Saint 110

Chapter 54. You Are the Salt of the Earth 112

Chapter 55. You Are Sealed Through Salvation 114

Chapter 56. You Share in Christ's Suffering 116

Chapter 57. You Are the Temple of the Holy Spirit 118

Chapter 58. You Are Washed 120

Chapter 59. You Have Wisdom and Revelation 122

Chapter 60. You Are His Workmanship............................. 124

YOU ARE ADOPTED

As you read Day 1: "You Are Adopted" in *Your True Reflection*, reflect on, and respond to the text by answering the following questions.

What does being adopted into God's family mean?

_____

_____

_____

_____

Do you see yourself as an adopted child of God? How does this influence you in your daily life? Consider your inner dialogue with your family, your job, your church, and your relationships.

_____

_____

_____

_____

How can you reconcile feelings of unworthiness with the knowledge that you are legally accepted into God's family? How does thinking about your adoption as a legal contract change the way you see and understand this concept?

_____

_____

_____

_____

How does the concept of earthy adoption and family shape your understanding of divine adoption?

_____

_____

_____

_____

Think of a time when you felt that God was far away. How did you respond to that feeling of distance or separation from your Heavenly Father? Why do you think you responded that way?

_____

_____

_____

What aspects of your life do you think would change if you saw yourself as an adopted child of the Most High? In what ways would your relationships, your career, and your health look different?

_____

_____

_____

How can you live in a way that reflects your identity as a child of God? Consider your answer. Does this line up with how you are living now?

_____

_____

_____

> *"For you have not received a spirit of slavery leading to fear again, but you have received a spirit of adoption as sons and daughters by which we cry out, 'Abba! Father!'"*
> —Romans 8:15 (NASB)

How often do you experience fear? Jot down some places in your life where fear seems to reoccur. In what ways does fear keep you from living life as if you belong to God?

_____

_____

_____

Consider the phrase "spirit of adoption". What does that mean to you? What is the difference between knowing you are an adopted child of God and embodying the spirit of adoption?

_____

_____

_____

STUDY 1 DAY 2

YOU HAVE ACCESS TO THE FATHER

As you read Day 2: "You Have Access to the Father" in *Your True Reflection*, reflect on, and respond to the text by answering the following questions.

In your own words, describe what it means to have "access" to your Heavenly Father. Why and how is it different than the access our ancestors before us had?

_____

_____

_____

_____

Describe a time—maybe one of the hardest times in your life—when you sought God the most. Re-imagine what that experience would have been like if God had not been there with you.

_____

_____

_____

_____

Knowing that He has given you direct, 24/7 access to Him, how does that change your approach to prayer? What would prayer have felt like back in the days of ancient Israel?

_____

_____

_____

_____

Tap into your imagination and think about the gift of having access to your Father. What images come to mind? What do you see in your mind's eye? What does that feel like?

_____

_____

_____

_____

8 | YOU HAVE ACCESS TO THE FATHER

How would your life change if you woke up and suddenly realized that you could not sit in the presence of God unless you traveled to a Temple?

_____

_____

_____

_____

Think about the story of Esther. How do you think God uses the access He's given us to position us in the right places at the right time?

_____

_____

_____

_____

> *For through him we both have access to the Father by one Spirit. Consequently, you are no longer foreigners and strangers, but fellow citizens with God's people and also members of the household of God.*
>
> **—Ephesians 2:18-19 (NIV)**

What does it mean to be a foreigner or stranger of God, from your perspective? What do you think that means from God's perspective?

_____

_____

_____

_____

Think about your own household (your relationship with your family members, the ways things are run in the home, your daily interactions). How are these dynamics similar or different than that of God's household with other believers?

_____

_____

_____

_____

YOU ARE ALIVE

As you read Day 3: "You Are Alive" in *Your True Reflection*, reflect on, and respond to the text by answering the following questions.

Why is it so powerful to know that we are "alive" in God but "dead" to sin?

_____

_____

_____

_____

Do you ever wrestle with confusion about why you wrestle with your flesh if you are made alive with Christ? How do you reconcile this tension?

_____

_____

_____

_____

Think about a time when you have felt spiritually dead in Christ but alive in the old man. How did you navigate that tension between the pull of your flesh and the pull of the Spirit? What do you do when your crucified self feels like it is overpowering your resurrected self? What are some ways you can overcome that?

_____

_____

_____

_____

If you lived every day like Christ dwelled within you, how would you approach and pursue your hopes, dreams, and aspirations? How would it affect your prayer life?

_____

_____

_____

_____

Think about where you are right now in your walk with Christ. Would Jesus say you are living a life fully and completely alive in Him? If not, how could you partner with Him to discover the fullness of His life that He intends for you to live?

_____

_____

_____

_____

How would living a life truly alive in God influence your perspective on physical death?

_____

_____

_____

_____

> *To you, who were spiritually dead all the time that you drifted along on the stream of this world's ideas of living, and obeyed its unseen ruler (who is still operating in those who do not respond to the truth of God), to you Christ has given life!*
> **—Ephesians 2:1 (Phillips)**

Think of some ways in the past that you have drifted along the stream of this world's ideas of living. What about right now? Why do you think that is?

_____

_____

_____

_____

_____

Think of some times in the past when you have felt truly alive in the Spirit. What did it feel like? How could you create more of that in your life now?

_____

_____

_____

_____

_____

YOU ARE APPOINTED TO SERVE

As you read Day 4: "You Are Appointed to Serve" in *Your True Reflection*, reflect on, and respond to the text by answering the following questions.

How do you feel about servanthood? Do you see yourself as a servant of God? Do you feel any resistance to being a servant of God? Why or why not?

_____

_____

_____

_____

What does it feel like to know that God has chosen you to make an impact on the Kingdom through serving others? Do you believe that God will equip you with whatever you need for wherever He sends you?

_____

_____

_____

_____

Can you think of a time when you have laid down your own needs and desires to serve someone else? How did you feel afterward?

_____

_____

_____

_____

How do you maintain a heart of service even when it feels difficult or thankless?

_____

_____

_____

_____

Do you feel like God can use you to build the Kingdom? How do you think He is using you now? In what ways do you think He wants to use you?

_____

_____

_____

How does serving others impact your understanding of God's calling on your life?

_____

_____

_____

> *I thank him who has given me strength, Christ Jesus our Lord, because he judged me faithful, appointing me to his service, though formerly I was a blasphemer, persecutor, and insolent opponent. But I received mercy because I had acted ignorantly in unbelief.*
>
> —1 Timothy 1:12-13

What do you think it was like for Paul to go from a persecutor of Christians to God's appointed servant of the Church? What would that be like for you? What would it feel like if God completely changed your heart tomorrow? How would you respond?

_____

_____

_____

Reflect on the progression of your walk with Jesus and describe a few times when you noticed Jesus was molding your heart to become His faithful servant. In what ways has the Lord softened your heart to lay your life down for others, and how has that shifted your own life?

_____

_____

_____

_____

How are unbelief and servanthood related?

_____

_____

_____

YOU ARE BLAMELESS

As you read Day 5: "You Are Blameless" in *Your True Reflection*, reflect on, and respond to the text by answering the following questions.

How does knowing that God sees you as blameless affect your self-view? Do you see yourself that way?

_____

_____

_____

_____

_____

_____

In what ways does being blameless before God impact your understanding of grace and mercy? To what degree do you find God's grace over your life show up in your transgression, sin, and iniquity?

_____

_____

_____

_____

_____

_____

How would knowing that God has deemed you blameless affect how you approach Him in prayer? How would it affect your response to mistakes and setbacks?

_____

_____

_____

_____

_____

_____

If you are blameless before God, then what does that mean about how we are to treat others who are made in God's image? Do you extend the grace to others that God is extending to you? List some examples.

_____

_____

_____

_____

What does living as a blameless individual look like practically in everyday life?

_____

_____

_____

_____

> *". . . that you may be blameless and innocent, children of God without blemish in the midst of a crooked and twisted generation, among whom you shine as lights in the world . . ."*
> **—Philippians 2:15**

Do you think it was difficult for Paul to accept that God viewed him as blameless before Him, given his active participation in that crooked and twisted generation?? Do you think Paul had to wrestle with shame and guilt in order to embrace God's judgment of him as innocent? What role does guilt and shame play in your own life?

_____

_____

_____

_____

_____

If you could walk through life with the assurance that you are without blemish, how would that encourage others to walk through their life as if they are without blemish?

_____

_____

_____

_____

_____

YOU ARE BLESSED

As you read Day 6: "You Are Blessed" in *Your True Reflection*, reflect on, and respond to the text by answering the following questions.

How would you define God's blessings, in your own words?

_____

_____

_____

_____

Can you think of a time when you felt blessed by God? What happened? What did you do with the blessing?

_____

_____

_____

_____

What do you think it means to be blessed with every good thing that belongs to Him? What does that say about who you are?

_____

_____

_____

_____

How have you navigated times when you felt devoid of blessings? How did it change your perspective of God? Of yourself?

_____

_____

_____

_____

_____

Do you think that you ever miss all that God has blessed you with? Do you recognize it? How often do you stop to consider all of the blessings God has bestowed upon you?

_____

_____

_____

_____

What do you think seeing yourself as blessed by God does for your self-image? Write down 10 ways in which God has showered His blessings upon you and take it in prayer.

_____

_____

_____

_____

> *Blessed be the God and Father of our Lord Jesus Christ, who has blessed us in Christ with every spiritual blessing in the heavenly places.*
>
> **—Ephesians 1:3**

The Scripture describes God as a "blessed" Father who has given us His blessings. In what ways do you think God is blessed? What does this mean about the blessings He has given you?

_____

_____

_____

_____

What is the difference between a spiritual blessing and an earthly blessing? How are they related? List an example of each and think about how God moves on your behalf in heavenly places and on earth.

_____

_____

_____

_____

_____

YOU ARE BROUGHT NEAR

As you read Day 7: "You Are Brought Near" in *Your True Reflection*, reflect on, and respond to the text by answering the following questions.

What does nearness to God look like?

_____

_____

_____

_____

How did Jesus's bloodshed bring us near to God? What is it about the blood that reconciled us back to the Father?

_____

_____

_____

_____

_____

When is the furthest you have ever felt from God? When did you realize that He was actually closer to you than your very breath?

_____

_____

_____

_____

When is the closest you have ever felt to God? What does that feel like and look like?

_____

_____

_____

_____

In your own words, explain why God's nearness transcends your feelings of distance between you and Him.

_____

_____

_____

_____

_____

Think about someone in your life who is not a believer. In what ways do their lives demonstrate a separation from God? What have you observed?

_____

_____

_____

_____

_____

> *"Let your gentle spirit be known to all people. The Lord is near."*
> **—Philippians 4:5 (NASB)**

How might a gentle spirit serve as evidence of the nearness of God to others who are seeking Him? How does it communicate a special relationship with Him?

_____

_____

_____

_____

_____

In what ways is the nearness of the Lord a powerful incentive to display gentleness to others—one of the many fruits of the Spirit?

_____

_____

_____

_____

_____

YOU ARE BUILT

As you read Day 8: "You Are Built" in *Your True Reflection*, reflect on, and respond to the text by answering the following questions.

How do you perceive the role of God as your "builder"? How does it provide comfort and guidance?

_____

_____

_____

_____

_____

How can you discern whether your foundation is built on solid rock or on shifting sand? Where do you find yourself right now? Why?

_____

_____

_____

_____

_____

What does it mean for you to be "complete" in Him?

_____

_____

_____

_____

_____

How do you respond when the building process feels challenging or uncomfortable?

_____

_____

_____

_____

In what ways have you experienced God "building" upon the foundation you've set in your life? Do you ever feel like God is building you too slowly? Too quickly?

_____

_____

_____

_____

_____

In what ways can you actively collaborate with God in the building process?

_____

_____

_____

_____

_____

> *Unless the LORD builds the house, those who build it labor in vain.*
> **—Psalm 127:1**

What comes to mean when you hear "labor in vain"? In what areas of your life have you experienced laboring in vain when the Lord wasn't the builder?

_____

_____

_____

_____

_____

What happens when you try to build yourself? What kind of things do you do? What is the end result?

_____

_____

_____

_____

_____

YOU ARE BURIED WITH CHRIST

As you read Day 9: "You Are Buried with Christ" in *Your True Reflection*, reflect on, and respond to the text by answering the following questions.

Have you been baptized? What did it feel like for you going under the water, and what did it feel like when you came out of the water?

_____

_____

_____

_____

What personal significance does baptism hold for you in relation to being buried with Christ?

_____

_____

_____

_____

How does understanding spiritual circumcision deepen your appreciation for Christ's work in your life? How does it magnify the death and resurrection of Jesus Christ?

_____

_____

_____

_____

What role does baptism play in your personal testimony and faith journey? Have you ever shared this testimony with anyone? How did they respond?

_____

_____

_____

_____

_____

If our old man was nailed to the cross, why does it sometimes feel like we have to kill the old every day? How do you reconcile that?

How can you communicate the importance of being buried with Christ and its implications to someone new to faith?

> *In him also you were circumcised with a circumcision made without hands, by putting off the body of the flesh, by the circumcision of Christ, having been buried with him in baptism, in which you were also raised with him through faith in the powerful working of God, who raised him from the dead. And you, who were dead in your trespasses and the uncircumcision of your flesh, God made alive together with him, having forgiven us all our trespasses.*
>
> **—Colossians 2:11-13**

How does this passage shape your understanding and appreciation of God's forgiveness and the life He offers? What does it mean for your freedom?

What do you think it should feel like to be made alive together with Christ? To what degree are your day-to-day experiences aligning with this feeling?

YOU ARE CHOSEN

As you read Day 10: "You Are Chosen" in *Your True Reflection*, reflect on, and respond to the text by answering the following questions.

How do you reconcile the concept of being chosen with the gift of free will?

_____

_____

_____

_____

What emotions and thoughts arise when you reflect on being chosen without having done anything to earn it?

_____

_____

_____

_____

Do you or have you ever fallen into the trap of a works-based life? Provide an example. Why do you think that doesn't bring joy and fulfillment?

_____

_____

_____

_____

_____

How would your life change if you were to live as if God loves you despite your imperfections, rather than striving to obtain His love?

_____

_____

_____

_____

Recall a time when you were given several options but then had to make a choice. Why did you choose it over the other options? How does knowing that God made a choice, and He chose you, shape your self-worth and identity?

_____

_____

_____

_____

In what ways does the culture of our world teach you that love, acceptance, and status are earned? How do you combat that narrative? How do you take the narrow path in the face of pressure to conform to the patterns of this world?

_____

_____

_____

_____

> *Even as he chose us in him before the foundation of the world, that we should be holy and blameless before him.—Ephesians 1:4*
>
> **—Ephesians 1:4**

Why do you think God chose you? How does this Scripture impact your understanding of God's love and intentionality towards you?

_____

_____

_____

_____

_____

What does it mean to be "chosen IN Him"?

_____

_____

_____

_____

_____

YOU ARE A CHILD OF GOD

As you read Day 11: "You Are a Child of God" in *Your True Reflection*, reflect on, and respond to the text by answering the following questions.

What unique qualities and privileges come with being a child of God that aren't found in early parent-child relationships?

_____

_____

_____

_____

Have you ever found yourself projecting your relationship with your parents onto the character of God? In what ways is your relationship with God different than your relationship with your parents?

_____

_____

_____

_____

Why might the world struggle to recognize the children of God, and how can you begin to reveal yourself as a child of God to the world?

_____

_____

_____

_____

What responsibilities come with being a child of the Almighty God? Do you feel equipped to fulfill those responsibilities? Why or why not?

_____

_____

_____

_____

How do you perceive God's discipline in your life as a loving Father?

_____

_____

_____

_____

If you were to ask God what it means to Him that you are his beloved child, what do you think He would say?

_____

_____

_____

_____

> *See what kind of love the Father has given to us, that we should be called children of God; and so we are. The reason why the world does not know us is that it did not know him. Beloved, we are God's children now, and what we will has not yet appeared; but we know that when he appears we shall be like him, because we shall see him as he is. And everyone who thus hopes in him purifies himself as he is pure.*
>
> —1 John 3:1-3

In what ways have you felt "unseen" or "unknown" by the world? How has that impacted you?

_____

_____

_____

_____

_____

Why do you think hope in the Lord takes us through a purification process? In what ways would you like to see greater purity in your life?

_____

_____

_____

_____

_____

YOU ARE A CITIZEN

As you read Day 12: "You Are a Citizen" in *Your True Reflection*, reflect on, and respond to the text by answering the following questions.

In what ways does heavenly citizenship offer a sense of belonging that transcends societal acceptance? Do you ever find yourself searching for belonging or acceptance outside of God?

_____

_____

_____

_____

How do you find balance between your roles and responsibilities on earth and your citizenship in heaven? How well do you think you find that balance?

_____

_____

_____

_____

How should our conduct in Christ look different than those who do not know God because of Who we belong to and where we belong?

_____

_____

_____

_____

What kind of promises do we have because of our citizenship in heaven that we wouldn't otherwise have?

_____

_____

_____

_____

In what ways does eternal life limit the scope of what it means to have heavenly citizenship? What does it offer for us here on earth?

_____

_____

_____

_____

Since you are a citizen of heaven, what does that say about God's trust in you to bring His will to earth?

_____

_____

_____

_____

> *So then you are no longer strangers and aliens, but you are fellow citizens with the saints and members of the household of God.*
>
> **—Ephesians 2:19**

What do you think Paul means when he says that you are a fellow citizen with the saints and members of the household of God?

_____

_____

_____

_____

_____

Compare the permanency of your citizenship in your country to the citizenship you have in heaven. What are the key differences? Do you feel like you are a citizen of heaven?

_____

_____

_____

_____

_____

_____

YOU ARE CONTENT IN YOUR SUFFICIENCY

**As you read Day 13: "You Are Content in Your Sufficiency"
in *Your True Reflection*, reflect on, and respond to the
text by answering the following questions.**

Are you satisfied with what you have in your life right now? Why or why not?

_____

_____

_____

_____

What DO you have right now that demonstrates God's sufficiency to provide you with everything you need to impact the Kingdom?

_____

_____

_____

_____

Do you ever battle with finding contentment? Why do you think that this? How can you find contentment when everything seems to be falling apart?

_____

_____

_____

_____

What kind of lessons have you learned from having little? What about when you've had much?

_____

_____

_____

_____

How does knowing that God has sufficiently provided you with all things oppose any limiting beliefs you have about yourself and your future?

_____

_____

_____

_____

How do you find confidence in the sufficiency of Christ amidst feelings of inadequacy?

_____

_____

_____

_____

> *Such is the confidence that we have through Christ toward God. Not that we are sufficient in ourselves to claim anything as coming from us, but our sufficiency is from God, who has made us sufficient to be ministers of a new covenant, not of the letter but of the Spirit. For the letter kills, but the Spirit gives life.*
>
> **—2 Corinthians 3:4–6**

In what ways do you see yourself as a minister of the new covenant? Why do you think God has chosen you to minister the new covenant to others?

_____

_____

_____

_____

_____

What does the Spirit do that the letter cannot do?

_____

_____

_____

_____

_____

YOU WEAR THE CROWN OF LIFE

As you read Day 14: "You Wear the Crown of Life" in *Your True Reflection*, reflect on, and respond to the text by answering the following questions.

When you think about the joy and bliss awaiting you in heaven, how does that reframe your perspective and experience of trials and tribulation?

_____

_____

_____

_____

Reflect on the challenges you face in fixing your mind on things eternal when you are under trial. What kind of thoughts do you have? What kind of stories do you tell yourself?

_____

_____

_____

_____

What would it look like to begin speaking God's promises of redemption and future hope over your life when you are anxious, insecure, depressed, or under pressure?

_____

_____

_____

_____

How are your trials indications of God's love and adoration for you? How do you think He views them?

_____

_____

_____

_____

How would you describe the difference between having or being given the crown of life and wearing it? Why is it so impactful to understand the difference?

_____

_____

_____

_____

In what ways are you living your life for earthly crowns, and in what ways are you living your life for crowns in heaven? What are some examples of each?

_____

_____

_____

_____

> *Blessed is the man who remains steadfast under trial, for when he has stood the test he will receive the crown of life, which God has promised to those who love him.*
>
> **—James 1:12**

Imagine yourself receiving a crown when you get to heaven. What do you think that crown represents? What images come to mind?

_____

_____

_____

_____

_____

_____

What trials are you walking through right now? Why is it important for us to endure trials in order to receive the crown of life?

_____

_____

_____

_____

_____

YOU ARE CRUCIFIED WITH CHRIST

**As you read Day 15: "You Are Crucified with Christ" in *Your True Reflection,*
reflect on, and respond to the text by answering the following questions.**

What parts of your flesh need to remain buried that keep surfacing in your life?

_____

_____

_____

_____

How do you respond when you notice temptation, sin, and shame begin to hover over
your life? What do you think God is inviting you to do in those moments?

_____

_____

_____

_____

What parts of you that died with Christ are difficult to let go of? Why do you think
that is?

_____

_____

_____

_____

How do you think the life of the Spirit inside you removes the appetites of your flesh
and replaces them with His? What do you need to do for that to happen?

_____

_____

_____

_____

What do you need to ask God for so that you can fully experience the life of Christ within you? What can you be praying for today?

_____

_____

_____

_____

Identify what is keeping you from experiencing the fullness of joy that is in the resurrected Christ within you. Look at your reflection in the mirror and tell yourself what Jesus wants for you. What did you say?

_____

_____

_____

_____

> *I have been crucified with Christ. It is no longer I who live, but Christ who lives in me. And the life I now live in the flesh I live by faith in the Son of God, who loved me and gave himself for me."*
>
> **—Galatians 2:20**

How does it make you feel to think that you no longer live? What would your life look like if you lived as if Christ was behind everything you did, said, and thought?

_____

_____

_____

_____

_____

Why do you think there is tension between your old self and your new identity in Christ? How could you still be a physical body while also living with the Spirit of Christ?

_____

_____

_____

_____

_____

_____

YOU ARE DEBT FREE

As you read Day 16: "You Are Debt Free" in *Your True Reflection*, reflect on, and respond to the text by answering the following questions.

In what ways are our sins considered debts? Why is that term used as a metaphor for our sins?

_____

_____

_____

_____

Can you think of someone in your life whose debt you would pay that you didn't accrue on your own? How much would you be willing to pay? Why? What do you think this says about the magnitude of Jesus's love for you?

_____

_____

_____

_____

What emotions or thoughts arise when you ponder the depth of love displayed in Jesus's cancelation of our debt?

_____

_____

_____

_____

How would you explain the cancelation of debt through the blood of Jesus to someone else who didn't understand it?

_____

_____

_____

_____

How could you leverage Jesus's sacrifice for forgiving others who have harmed you or violated you?

_____

_____

_____

_____

How can you honor and remember Jesus's sacrifice in your daily life and routines?

_____

_____

_____

_____

And you, who were dead in your trespasses and the uncircumcision of your flesh, God made alive together with him, having forgiven us all our trespasses, by canceling the record of debt that stood against us with its legal demands. This he set aside, nailing it to the cross.

—Colossians 2:13-14

Explain in your own words what it means to have your debts canceled. How do you make sense of that in light of spiritual debts versus financial debts?

_____

_____

_____

_____

_____

How does this Scripture influence your understanding of the cross and its significance in your life? If our debts were nailed to the cross, what should our day-to-day lives look like?

_____

_____

_____

_____

_____

_____

YOU ARE DELIVERED AND TRANSFERRED

**As you read Day 17: "You Are Delivered and Transferred"
in *Your True Reflection*, reflect on, and respond to the
text by answering the following questions.**

How has darkness shown up in your life?

_____

_____

_____

_____

Do you feel like you are still stuck in darkness? Explain why or why not.

_____

_____

_____

_____

How do you guard yourself against the temptations and remnants of the domain of darkness?

_____

_____

_____

_____

What have you done in the past that has opened your heart and mind up to darkness? What did you learn from that? How have your responses to temptation changed over time?

_____

_____

_____

_____

How has your transference to the kingdom of His beloved son shown up in your life? Have you ever shared your testimony with others? How would you share your testimony if you were asked to give it?

_____

_____

_____

_____

In what ways do you celebrate and remember your deliverance from darkness?

_____

_____

_____

_____

> *He has delivered us from the domain of darkness and transferred us to the kingdom of his beloved Son, in whom we have redemption, the forgiveness of sins.*
> —Colossians 1:13-14

What image comes to mind when you think of "deliverance" and "transference"?

_____

_____

_____

_____

_____

Reflect on a time in your life when God removed you from a dark place and then planted you in a place that gave you new hope and life. What did that experience show you about God? How did your relationship with Him grow?

_____

_____

_____

_____

_____

_____

YOU ARE ENTRUSTED WITH THE GOSPEL

**As you read Day 18: "You Are Entrusted with the Gospel"
in *Your True Reflection*, reflect on, and respond to the
text by answering the following questions.**

What challenges and responsibilities come with being entrusted with the gospel? Do
you have examples from your own life?

_____

_____

_____

_____

How do you ensure that your heart remains pure and untainted by personal biases and
worldly influence when you share the Good News?

_____

_____

_____

_____

Take some time to develop your own gospel-sharing message. What would you say?
How would you say it?

_____

_____

_____

_____

If you have shared the gospel already with someone else, how did you do it? Recount
the story. How would you teach others who have never shared the gospel before?

_____

_____

_____

_____

In what unique ways can you leverage your talents and platform to spread the gospel?

_____

_____

_____

_____

In what ways have you seen the impact of the gospel in the lives of those you've shared it with? How was your life impacted when someone shared the Good News with you?

_____

_____

_____

_____

For our appeal does not spring from error or impurity or any attempt to deceive, but just as we have been approved by God to be entrusted with the gospel, so we speak, not to please man, but to please God who tests our hearts.

—1 Thessalonians 2:3-4

What does Paul mean when he says that God tests our hearts? Why is the testing of our hearts necessary to faithfully and responsibly spread the message of the gospel?

_____

_____

_____

_____

_____

In what ways do you find yourself pleasing people instead of God? Why do you think Paul is encouraging us to only be concerned with the things that are pleasing to Him? What are the consequences of living a life devoted to pleasing people?

_____

_____

_____

_____

_____

YOU HAVE ETERNAL LIFE

As you read Day 19: "You Have Eternal Life" in *Your True Reflection*, reflect on, and respond to the text by answering the following questions.

In Matthew 6:19-20, Jesus instructs us to store our treasures in heaven and not on earth. What treasures are you storing up on earth? What about heaven?

_____

_____

_____

_____

What does it mean to you personally to possess the gift of eternal life now before reaching eternity?

_____

_____

_____

_____

Imagine your first face-to-face interaction with God in heaven. What is He saying to you? How are you responding? What do you feel?

_____

_____

_____

_____

What questions do you have about eternal life?

_____

_____

_____

_____

Does the promise of eternal life change the way you view death? Are you afraid of death?

_____

_____

_____

_____

What has God placed on your heart recently that will make you more and more like Jesus and prepare you for your seat in heaven?

_____

_____

_____

_____

> *And this is the testimony, that God gave us eternal life, and this life is in his Son. Whoever has the Son has life; whoever does not have the Son of God does not have life. I write these things to you who believe in the name of the Son of God, that you may know that you have eternal life.*
>
> —1 John 5:11–13

How does having eternal life affect your life here on earth? How can you bring heaven to earth where you find hell? When have you witnessed heaven being brought to earth? How did that feel?

_____

_____

_____

_____

_____

What do think the differences are between believing in the name of the Son of God and walking as if all that He has promised you now and forever is established, true, and unwavering?

_____

_____

_____

_____

YOU ARE FEARLESS

As you read Day 20: "You Are Fearless" in *Your True Reflection*, reflect on, and respond to the text by answering the following questions.

Do you know what it feels like to be bound up in fear? Where was the fear coming from? What was causing it?

_____

_____

_____

_____

How do you discern between healthy concerns and debilitating fears in your life?

_____

_____

_____

_____

Can you think of a time when God delivered you from a fear that you weren't sure would ever go away? Recount the story.

_____

_____

_____

_____

What kind of voices do you surround yourself with in your community? Is anyone speaking fear into your life?

_____

_____

_____

_____

How can you begin to exercise the authority God has given you over the enemy when he tries to accuse you and plant seeds of doubt about God's faithfulness in your heart?

_____

_____

_____

_____

How can you fortify your mind against fears and anxieties using the Word of God?

_____

_____

_____

_____

> *Do not be anxious about anything, but in everything by prayer and supplication with thanksgiving let your requests be made known to God. And the peace of God, which surpasses all understanding, will guard your hearts and your minds in Christ Jesus.*
>
> **—Philippians 4:6-7**

Why do you think God asks for your thanksgiving in your prayer time? Why is this a key part of experiencing God's peace?

_____

_____

_____

_____

_____

Can you think of a time when the peace of God surpassed your understanding in the middle of tumult and chaos? What did you notice was different about your thoughts? Your heart? Your behavior? Your words?

_____

_____

_____

_____

_____

YOU ARE FORGIVEN

As you read Day 21: "You Are Forgiven" in *Your True Reflection*, reflect on, and respond to the text by answering the following questions.

Do you see yourself the way God sees you—worthy of forgiveness? Why or why not?

_____
_____
_____
_____
_____

Why do you think God places such a strong emphasis on forgiveness in our relationship with Him?

_____
_____
_____
_____
_____

Why do you think it is so hard to forgive someone who has wronged us? What are we trying to accomplish by holding grudges?

_____
_____
_____
_____
_____

Have you ever had someone close to you extend their forgiveness to you even when you didn't deserve it? How did that make you feel?

_____
_____
_____

_____

_____

_____

How can you cultivate a heart that readily seeks and accepts God's forgiveness and graciously extends forgiveness to others?

_____

_____

_____

_____

What do you think embracing God's forgiveness for your sins could do for your life? Your relationships?

_____

_____

_____

_____

> *Be kind to one another, tenderhearted, forgiving one another, just as God in Christ forgave you.*
>
> **—Ephesians 4:32**

Have you ever found it difficult to forgive someone? Do you still have unforgiveness in your heart toward someone? How is it impacting you? How do you think it is impacting that person?

_____

_____

_____

_____

How could you begin to release unforgiveness today? What request could you bring to God to help you?

_____

_____

_____

_____

YOU ARE FREE

As you read Day 22: "You Are Free" in *Your True Reflection*, reflect on, and respond to the text by answering the following questions.

Describe a time in your life when you felt the freest. Who were you with? What were you doing? What was your relationship with God like at the time?

_____

_____

_____

_____

How do you personally define the freedom you have in Christ? Do you think your definition lines up with His? Why or why not?

_____

_____

_____

_____

Think about an area of your life where you are living as if you are still captive to the world (family, friendships, work, financially, etc.). What do you think is keeping you captive?

_____

_____

_____

_____

Think about areas of your life where you are truly living in the freedom given to us in Christ. What does that freedom look like? How can you apply that freedom to other areas of bondage?

_____

_____

_____

_____

In what ways have you personally experienced the dangers of misusing your freedom to satisfy fleshly desires? How did God's grace show up for you?

_____

_____

_____

_____

What is the difference between being a slave to the world and a slave to Christ? What is your knee-jerk reaction to "slave"? How is it that it is in slavery to Christ that you are truly free?

_____

_____

_____

_____

> *For you were called to freedom, brothers. Only do not use your freedom*
> *as an opportunity for the flesh, but through love serve one another.*
> **—Galatians 5:13**

In what ways do we sometimes abuse our freedom in Christ to pursue our own fleshly desires?

_____

_____

_____

_____

_____

How do you ensure that your freedom in Christ is used for love and service, and not selfish desires?

_____

_____

_____

_____

_____

YOU ARE GIFTED

As you read Day 23: "You Are Gifted" in *Your True Reflection*, reflect on, and respond to the text by answering the following questions.

Have you ever taken a strengths or spiritual gifts assessment? What are some of the unique giftings God has given you?

_____

_____

_____

_____

What gifts do others see in you? What have you been told by close friends, family, or Christian mentors? Do you agree or disagree with them? Why or why not?

_____

_____

_____

_____

On a scale from 1-10 (1 = not at all clear, 10 = extremely clear), how clear are you on your God-given gifts and how He wants you to use them?

_____

_____

_____

_____

Of the three types of gifts listed in this devotional (motivational gifts, situational gifts, equipping gifts), which of them resonates with you most? Explain.

_____

_____

_____

_____

Do you ever struggle with comparing the size or quantity of your gifts with others? How do you navigate feelings of inadequacy or comparison when it comes to spiritual gifts?

_____

_____

_____

_____

Who in your life (family, friend, counselor, pastor) can you talk to help you discover and refine the giftings God has deposited within you?

_____

_____

_____

_____

> *Having gifts that differ according to the grace given to us, let us use them. . . .*
> **—Romans 12:6**

How do you discern and validate the gifts given to you according to the grace of God? Have you ever received God's confirmation of your giftings?

_____

_____

_____

_____

_____

_____

In what ways are you currently using or can you better use your gifts for the Kingdom? What kind of direction has God given you?

_____

_____

_____

_____

_____

_____

_____

YOU HAVE GRACE

As you read Day 24: "You Have Grace" in *Your True Reflection*, reflect on, and respond to the text by answering the following questions.

How is grace different than mercy? Define each one.

_____

_____

_____

_____

Given this understanding of grace, what kind of experiences have you had with God's grace?

_____

_____

_____

_____

Do you have a difficult time embracing and receiving God's grace over your life? What in your past or present are you holding onto that is already covered by the blood of Jesus?

_____

_____

_____

_____

How does understanding that blessings as God's unmerited favor over you influence your response to successes and failures?

_____

_____

_____

_____

How do you navigate societal pressures to take credit for achievements and accomplishments? In what ways have your successes been a direct result of God's grace?

_____

_____

_____

_____

How does earning your way to success and acceptance pervert the gospel of grace? What message does that send about Jesus's love for you?

_____

_____

_____

_____

> *But by the grace of God I am what I am, and His grace toward me did not prove vain; but I labored even more than all of them, yet not I, but the grace of God with me*
>
> **—1 Corinthians 15:10, (NASB)**

In what ways have you experienced God's grace enabling you to labor and serve beyond your capacity? Describe.

_____

_____

_____

_____

_____

What is the greatest thing you've ever achieved in your life? Looking back, how was God's strength and grace behind it?

_____

_____

_____

_____

_____

YOU ARE HEARD

As you read Day 25: "You Are Heard" in *Your True Reflection*, reflect on, and respond to the text by answering the following questions.

What do you think the difference is between listening and hearing?

_____

_____

_____

_____

Have you ever felt like God does not hear you? What made you feel that way?

_____

_____

_____

_____

How do you think God responds when He hears your requests, your triumphs, and your bids for rescue?

_____

_____

_____

_____

If God always hears us, why do you think He sometimes feels absent? Describe a time when you felt like God was silent. When did He break His silence? How does that give you hope for your future?

_____

_____

_____

_____

What kind of daily practices could you begin to implement that would help you hear the voice of God? What does your "God time" look like right now?

_____

_____

_____

_____

How do you interpret God's silence?

_____

_____

_____

_____

> *And this is the confidence that we have toward him, that if we ask anything according to his will he hears us. And if we know that he hears us in whatever we ask, we know that we have the requests that we have asked of him.*
>
> **—1 John 5:14-15**

Are you asking God everything that is on your heart to ask? Do you believe that He is attentive to every request? What do you think holds you back from asking Him what you need?

_____

_____

_____

_____

_____

_____

What does it mean to ask "according to His will"? Do you have any prayers in your life that have gone unanswered? Do you believe that they will be answered?

_____

_____

_____

_____

_____

YOU ARE THE HEIR OF ALL THINGS

As you read Day 26: "You Are the Heir of All Things" in *Your True Reflection*, reflect on, and respond to the text by answering the following questions.

Is it difficult for you to see yourself as an heir of all of the things of God? Why or why not?

_____

_____

_____

_____

Do you ever feel like God is withholding something from you? What do you feel like He is keeping from you? Why do you feel that way?

_____

_____

_____

_____

Do you tend to view God as a punisher, a grace-giving, loving God, or somewhere in between? Give some examples from your own life.

_____

_____

_____

_____

God has already given you every single treasured possession of His—everything on earth and in heaven. What does that say about your authority over darkness?

_____

_____

_____

_____

What does being an heir of all things enable us to do in this life?

_____

_____

_____

_____

What is the enemy trying to accomplish through his lies that you are worthless or have nothing that God wants? What is he trying to convince you to believe about yourself and about God? How do you combat those lies?

_____

_____

_____

_____

> *SHis divine power has granted to us all things that pertain to life and godliness, through the knowledge of him who called us to his own glory and excellence, by which he has granted to us his precious and very great promises, so that through them you may become partakers of the divine nature, having escaped from the corruption that is in the world because of sinful desire.*
>
> **—2 Peter 1:3-4**

How would you describe what it means that He has called us to His own glory and excellence through the knowledge of Him?

_____

_____

_____

_____

_____

How does our inheritance of all things save us from worldly corruption and evil? What is the connection between the two?

_____

_____

_____

_____

_____

YOU ARE HIDDEN IN CHRIST

As you read Day 27: "You Are Hidden in Christ" in *Your True Reflection*, reflect on, and respond to the text by answering the following questions.

Do you ever feel exposed and vulnerable before God when you sin? In what ways can you relate to Adam and Eve's response to their disobedience in the garden?

_____

_____

_____

_____

Why do you think it's essential to approach God with transparency, without hiding your sins or your shame?

_____

_____

_____

_____

Do you have any testimonies of God's kindness and deliverance when you have allowed Him to find you?

_____

_____

_____

_____

What kind of thoughts do you rehearse in your head when you have sinned? How do you think God would respond to those thoughts? What is HE saying to you?

_____

_____

_____

_____

What does running away from God feel like? How does it serve you?

_____

_____

_____

_____

What would happen if you chose to run toward Him instead?

_____

_____

_____

_____

> *You are a hiding place for me; you preserve me from trouble;*
> *you surround me with shouts of deliverance.*
>
> **—Psalm 32:7**

Reflect on a time in your life when God has protected you from destruction. How does that impact your understanding of being "hidden" in Christ?

_____

_____

_____

_____

_____

_____

What does it look like to run to God and hide in Him rather than hide from Him? How do you tend to respond when you have sinned?

_____

_____

_____

_____

_____

_____

YOU ARE HOLY AND MADE COMPLETE

**As you read Day 28: "You Are Holy and Made Complete"
in *Your True Reflection*, reflect on, and respond to the
text by answering the following questions.**

In what ways do you actively seek guidance from the Holy Spirit to grow in holiness?

_____

_____

_____

How does the knowledge of the Holy Spirit's presence impact your daily decisions and behaviors?

_____

_____

_____

Reflect on your journey with the Lord over the past five years. How has God made you more sensitive to the voice and leading of the Spirit?

_____

_____

_____

Do you ever find yourself relying on your own strength to accomplish the work of the Kingdom? In what ways?

_____

_____

_____

What does it look like to "work out our faith practically while we are here"? What is our part to play?

_____

_____

_____

How would you describe the process of active collaboration with the Holy Spirit to grow in holiness and godliness?

_____

_____

_____

_____

_____

_____

Therefore, holy brothers, you who share in a heavenly calling,
consider Jesus, the apostle and high priest of our confession..
—**Hebrews 3:1**

Refer back to the Greek meaning of "holy" in today's devotional. How would you describe your life as "set apart"? In what ways have you found yourself fulfilling your identity as set apart?

_____

_____

_____

_____

_____

And I am sure of this, that he who began a good work in you
will bring it to completion at the day of Jesus Christ.
—**Philippians 1:6**

What do you think it will look like to one day be a completed work? What do you think God is perfecting in your heart right now?

_____

_____

_____

_____

_____

STUDY 6 DAY 29

YOU ARE A LAVISHED CHILD OF GOD

As you read Day 29: "You Are a Lavished Child of God" in *Your True Reflection*, reflect on, and respond to the text by answering the following questions.

Today's devotional defines "lavished" as being over and above, to abound or overflow, or to be left over. Provide some examples of how God shows up lavishly in our lives.

_____

_____

_____

_____

Think about the story of the wave runner tour. What do you think God wants you to do when He blesses you with overflow?

_____

_____

_____

_____

_____

Why do you think God wants to bless us lavishly? Why isn't it enough for Him to just adopt us as His children?

_____

_____

_____

_____

_____

How does your identity as a lavished child of God differ from how you see yourself?

_____

_____

_____

_____

What does it look like to wait for and expect God's abundance?

_____

_____

_____

_____

How can you daily remind yourself of God's unwavering love and the blessings you've received as His lavished child?

_____

_____

_____

_____

> *See what great love the Father has lavished on us, that we should be called children of God! And that is what we are! The reason the world does not know us is that it did not know him.*
>
> **—1 John 3:1 (NIV)**

When have you seen God go above and beyond your expectations, either for something you were praying for or a blessing you didn't ask for at all?

_____

_____

_____

_____

_____

Have you ever felt rejected or unseen by the world? What would change if you remembered who they were really rejecting (Jesus)?

_____

_____

_____

_____

_____

YOU ARE THE LIGHT OF THE WORLD

As you read Day 30: "You Are the Light of the World" in *Your True Reflection*, reflect on, and respond to the text by answering the following questions.

How can you continue to shine brightly even when you are feeling lost and overwhelmed?

_____

_____

_____

_____

Recall a time when someone else has been a light in the darkness for you. How did it make you feel? What kind of difference did it make? What kind of changes did you notice take place?

_____

_____

_____

_____

How does a person who shines the light of Jesus act? What words do they speak? What thoughts do they think?

_____

_____

_____

_____

How does a person living in darkness act? What words do they speak? What thoughts do they think?

_____

_____

_____

_____

What can you do when you feel like your light is being extinguished? How do we return to the light when we feel like we've drifted away?

_____

_____

_____

_____

How does God's commission for you to be a light to a dark world challenge you to shine brighter in your community and spheres of influence?

_____

_____

_____

_____

> *"You are the light of the world. A city set on a hill cannot be hidden. Nor do people light a lamp and put it under a basket, but on a stand, and it gives light to all in the house. In the same way, let your light shine before others, so that they may see your good works and give glory to your Father who is in heaven."*
> **—Matthew 5:14-16**

Do you ever feel like you have hidden your light from others? Why do you think that happened?

_____

_____

_____

_____

_____

_____

Why is it so important to give others the opportunity to see God in you and through you?

_____

_____

_____

_____

_____

_____

YOU ARE LOVED

As you read Day 31: "You Are Loved" in *Your True Reflection*, reflect on, and respond to the text by answering the following questions.

How is the love of God different than the love of man?

_____

_____

_____

_____

When did you experience the vastness and depth of God's love the most deeply? Can you explain what you felt?

_____

_____

_____

_____

_____

Do you ever feel numb to God's love? Why or why not?

_____

_____

_____

_____

Recall a time when you made a sacrifice for someone else. How did that make you feel? How did it make that person feel? How can you create more of those experiences?

_____

_____

_____

_____

_____

Do you find it challenging to love people who are difficult to love? What kind of patterns have you noticed that do not exemplify the love of Christ?

_____

_____

_____

_____

In contrast, how has God enabled you to love people who are difficult to love? Provide an example.

_____

_____

_____

_____

> *And you were dead in the trespasses and sins in which you once walked, following the course of this world, following the prince of the power of the air, the spirit that is now at work in the sons of disobedience—among whom we all once lived in the passions of our flesh, carrying out the desires of the body and the mind, and were by nature children of wrath, like the rest of mankind.*
>
> —Ephesians 2:1 (NASB)

Based on your own experiences and changes you have observed in others, what does transformation from walking in disobedience to living in God's grace look like?

_____

_____

_____

_____

What does it mean to be a "child of wrath"? What kind of differences do you see between children of wrath and children who are in Christ?

_____

_____

_____

_____

_____

_____

YOU HAVE MERCY

As you read Day 32: "You Have Mercy" in *Your True Reflection*, reflect on, and respond to the text by answering the following questions.

Reflect on a time when someone in your life showed you mercy. What kind of impact did that have on your relationship with that person?

_____

_____

_____

_____

In what specific ways have you personally experienced the mercy of God in your life?

_____

_____

_____

_____

How does recognizing God's mercy in your own life affect your interactions with others and your ability to extend mercy to them?

_____

_____

_____

_____

How does the depth of God's mercy influence your understanding of and approach to repentance and reconciliation?

_____

_____

_____

_____

How has God always been a merciful God, from the Old Testament to the New Testament? Can you think of some examples throughout the Old and New Testaments that demonstrate His mercy?

_____

_____

_____

_____

If someone you knew was battling with deep guilt or shame, how would you tell them about God's mercy to encourage them? What would you say?

_____

_____

_____

_____

> *But you are a chosen race, a royal priesthood, a holy nation, a people for his own possession, that you may proclaim the excellencies of him who called you out of darkness into his marvelous light. Once you were not a people, but now you are God's people; once you had not received mercy, but now you have received mercy.*
>
> **—1 Peter 2:9-10**

What do you think life, in light of living under the mercy of God, looks like before handing our lives over to Him versus after? Can you relate personally? Do you know someone who can?

_____

_____

_____

_____

_____

In this Scripture, Peter says, "Once you were not a people." What do you think that means?

_____

_____

_____

_____

_____

YOU ARE MORE THAN A CONQUEROR

As you read Day 33: "You Are More than a Conqueror" in *Your True Reflection*,
reflect on, and respond to the text by answering the following questions.

Think about something you have "conquered" in your life—maybe an obstacle, the
pain of a loss, or opposition. What did you learn from your victory?

_____
_____
_____
_____

In what ways was the hand of God in that victory? Where did you see Him?

_____
_____
_____
_____

How are we to approach spiritual warfare as more than conquerors in Christ?

_____
_____
_____
_____

What kind of lies or weapons of deceit have you encountered that argue against your
identity as a conqueror? What does the devil know about you that you don't?

_____
_____
_____
_____

Can you think of a time when you felt like you lost the battle against the enemy? A time
when you felt defeated, discouraged, or hopeless? Why do you think that happened?

_____

_____

_____

_____

Who in your life lives their life as more than a conqueror? What can you glean from them that will help you walk in your identity as a conqueror?

_____

_____

_____

_____

> *Who shall separate us from the love of Christ? Shall tribulation, or distress, or persecution, or famine, or nakedness, or danger, or sword? As it is written, 'For your sake we are being killed all the day long; we are regarded as sheep to be slaughtered.' No, in all these things we are more than conquerors through him who loved us."*
>
> —Romans 8:35–37

Considering the list of oppressive experiences that Paul presents in this Scripture, what would it feel like to be separated from the love of Christ as we endure trials?

_____

_____

_____

_____

_____

How do you dial into Christ's immense love for you when it feels like He is distant? Is there a time when you saw the love of Christ present during those times in hindsight?

_____

_____

_____

_____

_____

YOU ARE A NEW CREATION

**As you read Day 34: "You Are a New Creation" in *Your True Reflection*,
reflect on, and respond to the text by answering the following questions.**

What are some past mistakes you have made in your life that produce recurring shame
and regret, and how does being a new creation reframe these patterns?

_____

_____

_____

_____

What are some areas in your life where you need assurance from God that He has
already paved a new way for you?

_____

_____

_____

_____

How does living every day as if it's a new day differ from how you are living your life now?

_____

_____

_____

_____

Re-read the Greek definition of "new creation." One rendering of this term is "unused".
How do you interpret what it means to be unused in light of God's faithfulness and
unfailing love?

_____

_____

_____

_____

What parts of you is God waiting for you to perceive, accept, and receive that have already been re-created?

_____

_____

_____

_____

In what ways is holding onto your past preventing you from waking up each morning with joy in your heart that you have an opportunity for a fresh start that day?

_____

_____

_____

_____

> *Therefore, if anyone is in Christ, he is a new creation. The old has passed away; behold, the new has come.*
>
> **—2 Corinthians 5:17**

How has Christ renewed various aspects of your life, heart, and character? Provide some examples, including where you started and how He has re-shaped you.

_____

_____

_____

_____

_____

_____

Paul tells the people of Corinth that the old has passed away, and the new has come. What all has Christ ushered into the world that is new?

_____

_____

_____

_____

_____

YOU HAVE A NEW NAME

**As you read Day 35: "You Have a New Name" in *Your True Reflection*,
reflect on, and respond to the text by answering the following questions.**

What does it really mean to be given a new name? What is the significance of that for you?

_____

_____

_____

_____

What questions still linger about God's new name for you as an expression of His deep desire and love for you?

_____

_____

_____

_____

In what ways does having a new name in Christ symbolize your personal journey and relationship with God?

_____

_____

_____

_____

Why do you think God's name for you is different than God's name for anyone else?

_____

_____

_____

_____

What does your new name say about your devotion and surrender to Christ?

_____

_____

_____

_____

What names have you been given (or have given yourself) that have countered who God says you are, and what are some names that reflect the heart of God that might replace them?

_____

_____

_____

_____

He who has an ear, let him hear what the Spirit says to the churches. To the one who conquers I will give some of the hidden manna, and I will give him a white stone, with a new name written on the stone that no one knows except the one who receives it.

—Revelation 2:17

What name(s) do you think God has for you?

_____

_____

_____

_____

_____

_____

Why is it so special that the new name God has given you is private, just between you and Him?

_____

_____

_____

_____

_____

_____

YOU ARE NO LONGER CONDEMNED

As you read Day 36: "You Are No Longer Condemned" in *Your True Reflection*, reflect on, and respond to the text by answering the following questions.

Do you have personal experience with fear of condemnation? Describe.

_____

_____

_____

_____

Can you recall a moment when you truly felt free from condemnation? What was that like for you?

_____

_____

_____

_____

What does it mean to you to live unafraid and free to make mistakes, and how does this connect with your understanding of God's mercy?

_____

_____

_____

_____

In what areas of your life do you find it most challenging to accept that you have been freed from all shame, guilt, and condemnation? Why do you think that is?

_____

_____

_____

_____

Think about believers you know (this may be you) who struggle with shame or fear of punishment from God. Where do you think that comes from? What is at the root of that fear?

_____

_____

_____

_____

Who in the Bible (apart from Jesus) do you think embodied the freedom given to us in Christ through a life completely absent of fear of condemnation?

_____

_____

_____

_____

> "... when we are judged, we are disciplined by the Lord so that we will not be condemned along with the world."
>
> —1 Corinthians 11:32 (NASB)

Have you ever been disciplined by the Lord? How? How does the discipline of the Lord demonstrate His love and care for us, according to this verse?

_____

_____

_____

_____

_____

_____

How does God's discipline differ from condemnation? Why does discipline protect us from condemnation?

_____

_____

_____

_____

_____

_____

YOU ARE NO LONGER IN NEED

As you read Day 37: "You Are No Longer in Need" in *Your True Reflection*, reflect on, and respond to the text by answering the following questions.

Can you think of scripture that speaks to God's heart as your Provider, and how does that resonate with you?

_____

_____

_____

_____

In practical terms, what does it look like to live with the belief that all of your needs will be met because you are God's child?

_____

_____

_____

_____

How does the theme of God's provision challenge common cultural beliefs about independence and self-sufficiency?

_____

_____

_____

_____

Imagine you are uncertain about whether you'll be able to pay your rent next month. What would that look like if you believed it was all on your shoulders to come up with the money? What would it look like if you stood firm in your faith and trusted that God would shoulder some of that burden?

_____

_____

_____

_____

Reflect on a time when you doubted whether God would provide for a need. What helped you restore your trust?

_____

_____

_____

_____

How do you handle the pressure while you are waiting on God's provision?

_____

_____

_____

_____

> *And my God will supply every need of yours according to his riches in glory in Christ Jesus.*
> **—Philippians 4:19**

Think about a time when you were crippled by fear of lack and were desperate for God's provision. How did He come through for you? What can you take with you into your future from that experience?

_____

_____

_____

_____

_____

How do you define "needs"? What are some examples of "need"? What are some examples of "want"? In what ways do you think God provides us with our "wants", and in what ways does He not?

_____

_____

_____

_____

_____

_____

YOU ARE AN OVERCOMER

As you read Day 38: "You Are an Overcomer" in *Your True Reflection*, reflect on, and respond to the text by answering the following questions.

How does the idea of finding victory through surrender challenge common understandings of strength and power?

_____

_____

_____

_____

Can you think of a time when surrendering to God led to unexpected victory in your life?

_____

_____

_____

_____

How do you reconcile the defeat we often feel on our darkest nights with the truth that we have victory over that darkness?

_____

_____

_____

_____

_____

In what areas of your life do you find it most difficult to surrender control, and how might this be hindering your experience as an overcomer?

_____

_____

_____

_____

_____

What does it mean to you that victory comes through faith in Jesus, and not through our own efforts?

_____

_____

_____

_____

Practically, what does surrender look like in your relationship with God? Do you find surrender to be difficult? In what ways have you noticed growth in your ability to surrender?

_____

_____

_____

_____

> *For everyone who has been born of God overcomes the world. And this is the victory that has overcome the world—our faith. Who is it that overcomes the world except the one who believes that Jesus is the Son of God?*
>
> *—1 John 5:4-5*

In what ways has your faith been a source of victory in your life?

_____

_____

_____

_____

_____

_____

Why did it take Jesus's death on a cross and resurrection to afford us victory in every area of our lives?

_____

_____

_____

_____

_____

_____

YOU ARE OVERFLOWING WITH HOPE

As you read Day 39: "You Are Overflowing with Hope" in *Your True Reflection*, reflect on, and respond to the text by answering the following questions.

Why do you think Paul doesn't just say that we have hope in Christ, but are instead overflowing with hope?

_____

_____

_____

_____

Have you ever felt afraid to hope? Why or why not?

_____

_____

_____

_____

Why does God tell us that hope never disappoints? How can we reconcile this truth with times when prayers have gone unanswered or were answered in a way that we didn't expect or want?

_____

_____

_____

_____

Recall a time when your hope in God, particularly during a tough season, was fulfilled. What impact did that have on your faith?

_____

_____

_____

_____

What in your life are you still hoping for? Does anyone in your circle of influence know? How could you invite them to join you in prayer?

_____

_____

_____

_____

By and large, the concept of hope suggests the promise of a bright future. What does a bright future look like for you?

_____

_____

_____

_____

> *Having the eyes of your hearts enlightened, that you may know what is the hope to which he has called you, what are the riches of his glorious inheritance in the saints, and what is the immeasurable greatness of his power toward us who believe, according to the working of his great might.*
> —**Ephesians 1:18-19**

What does it mean for our hearts to be enlightened?

_____

_____

_____

_____

_____

_____

How does an enlightened heart provide us with knowledge of the hope we have in Him? What is that hope?

_____

_____

_____

_____

_____

_____

YOU ARE A PARTAKER

As you read Day 40: "You Are a Partaker" in *Your True Reflection*, reflect on, and respond to the text by answering the following questions.

Can you think of a time when you felt like a co-laborer with God in a specific situation? What was that like for you?

_____

_____

_____

_____

What role does humility play in our willingness to be co-laborers with God, and how can we cultivate a humble heart?

_____

_____

_____

_____

How can we discern God's invitation to join Him in His work, and how can we respond in obedience?

_____

_____

_____

_____

Can you think of a time when God gave you an opportunity to partake in His work and you ignored or walked away from the opportunity? Why do you think that happened?

_____

_____

_____

_____

Conversely, can you think of a time when God gave you an opportunity and you took it? What came out of that act of obedience?

_____

_____

_____

_____

Has God placed an invitation on your heart to partake with Him in some way? Where do you feel He is inviting you to?

_____

_____

_____

_____

> *His divine power has granted to us all things that pertain to life and godliness, through the knowledge of him who called us to his own glory and excellence, by which he has granted to us his precious and very great promises, so that through them you may become partakers of the divine nature, having escaped from the corruption that is in the world because of sinful desire.*
>
> —2 Peter 1:3-4

What does Peter mean when he says that we are not partakers of the divine nature?

_____

_____

_____

_____

_____

How is being a partaker in God's work different than simply being saved and sealed with the promise of eternal life?

_____

_____

_____

_____

_____

_____

YOU HAVE PEACE

As you read Day 41: "You Have Peace" in *Your True Reflection*, reflect on, and respond to the text by answering the following questions.

What does perfect peace feel like? How is it possible to have perfect peace even when everything around you seems anything but peaceful?

_____

_____

_____

_____

_____

Are you in perfect peace? Why or why not? Have you ever felt perfect peace in the middle of an unpeaceful situation?

_____

_____

_____

_____

_____

Have you ever looked for peace in something outside of God? Did you find it?

_____

_____

_____

_____

How does the peace that God offers differ from the fleeting peace the world offers?

_____

_____

_____

_____

Why do you think many people might not recognize that the peace they seek is found in God only?

_____

_____

_____

_____

How might your interaction with others change if you truly understood the depth of peace God offers?

_____

_____

_____

_____

> *For those who are in accord with the flesh set their minds on the things of the flesh, but those who are in accord with the Spirit, the things of the Spirit. For the mind set on the flesh is death, but the mind set on the Spirit is life and peace.*
>
> **—Romans 8:5-6 (NASB)**

How does setting your mind on the Spirit bring life and peace into your circumstances? What do you think the Word does for your mind that creates this peace?

_____

_____

_____

_____

In what practical ways can you shift your mindset from the flesh to the Spirit in daily life? If you could live a life with limitless peace, even in the midst of turmoil, what kind of person do you think you would be? How would your relationships change? Your confidence?

_____

_____

_____

_____

_____

YOU HAVE POWER

As you read Day 42: "You Have Power" in *Your True Reflection*, reflect on, and respond to the text by answering the following questions.

What does it mean to you to have power in Jesus Christ? What kind of power does Jesus have?

_____

_____

_____

_____

How do you navigate situations where you feel powerless, despite knowing the power available in Jesus? Do you ever try to rely on your power? How do you know when you are relying on your own strength and not God's?

_____

_____

_____

_____

In what ways does the power in Jesus Christ equip you for spiritual warfare? Have you ever done spiritual warfare when you were in a place of opposition? What was that like? What did you notice after?

_____

_____

_____

_____

Do you ever think of yourself as able to operate in the supernatural? Have you ever had an experience that boasted God's supernatural power?

_____

_____

_____

_____

_____

What do you think it would take for you to believe that you are a ruler in Jesus Christ, able to perform miracles beyond comprehension?

_____

_____

_____

_____

> *. . . and my speech and my message were not in plausible words of wisdom, but in demonstration of the Spirit and of power, so that your faith might not rest in the wisdom of men but in the power of God.*
>
> **—1 Corinthians 2:4-5**

Refer to the story of Joshua and the Ebenezer they built—twelve stacked stones. If you were to build your own Ebenezer, what would you write on each one to remind you of God's supernatural provision or His power at work within you made manifest?

_____

_____

_____

_____

_____

_____

To what extent do you rest on the wisdom of man? What kind of impact has that had on your life? When have you relied fully on the power of God, and what did you notice?

_____

_____

_____

_____

_____

_____

_____

YOU ARE PREDESTINED

As you read Day 43: "You Are Predestined" in *Your True Reflection*, reflect on, and respond to the text by answering the following questions.

How do you reconcile human free will with the doctrine of predestination?

_____

_____

_____

_____

What comfort and challenges do you find in knowing you were chosen before the foundation of the world? In ways does your life seem to align with this and in what ways doesn't it?

_____

_____

_____

_____

Do you remember the day you chose to follow Jesus? Recount that experience. What is your story? Why did you make that choice?

_____

_____

_____

_____

What kind of relationship do you envision someone who was chosen by Christ since the beginning would have with God?

_____

_____

_____

_____

When you feel discouraged or unworthy, how could remembering that you were handpicked by God to change your interpretation of your feelings? What steps can you take to push back against that?

_____

_____

_____

_____

Think about who you want to be in five, ten, thirty, and fifty years from now. How do envision yourself as being conformed to the image of Christ with each passing year?

_____

_____

_____

_____

> *. . . even as he chose us in him before the foundation of the world, that we should be holy and blameless before him.*
>
> **—Ephesians 1:4**

Why do you think God chose you before He even created the heavens and earth? Does this affect your sense of purpose and identity? How could you apply this truth to your life?

_____

_____

_____

_____

_____

What does a holy and blameless life look like to you?

_____

_____

_____

_____

_____

STUDY 9 DAY 44

YOU HAVE PRECIOUS AND GREAT PROMISES

**As you read Day 44: "You Have Precious and Great
Promises" in *Your True Reflection*, reflect on, and respond
to the text by answering the following questions.**

What promise in Scripture is particularly impactful and encouraging for you? Is there
a promise that you seem to recite and rehearse more than others? Why do you think it
resonates so much with you?

_____

_____

_____

_____

_____

In what ways have you experienced the fulfillment of God's promises in your life?

_____

_____

_____

_____

What does it mean to you personally to be a recipient of God's promises?

_____

_____

_____

_____

Have you ever lost faith in God because of an unfulfilled promise? How did that
impact your view of Him? How did it impact the way you think He feels about you?

_____

_____

_____

_____

Can you think of a time when you have looked back and understood why God made you wait for something? How did you come to understand His glory? How did it strengthen your faith in Him?

_____

_____

_____

_____

> *The Lord is not slow about His promise, as some count slowness, but is patient toward you, not willing for any to perish, but for all to come to repentance.*
> **—2 Peter 3:9 (NASB)**

How does this Scripture influence your understanding and response to the delay of God's promises? Do you ever lose heart when you receive a promise from God but haven't seen it come to pass? Why do you think God sometimes makes us wait?

_____

_____

_____

_____

_____

_____

_____

Take note of a promise that you have been waiting to come to pass for a long time. What could you bring to the Lord in prayer today about this desire? How does the waiting period reflect God's love and care for you?

_____

_____

_____

_____

_____

_____

_____

_____

YOU ARE RAISED WITH CHRIST

As you read Day 45: "You Are Raised with Christ" in *Your True Reflection*, reflect on, and respond to the text by answering the following questions.

What does it really mean to walk in newness of life, having been raised with Christ? How would your interactions, attitude, and work look different if you were walking in newness of life?

_____

_____

_____

_____

_____

_____

How do you experience the resurrection power of Christ in your daily life? Contrast what it feels like to walk in your old life versus walking in the new life Christ gave you.

_____

_____

_____

_____

_____

_____

In what areas of your life could you use a little "newness"? Why do you think it is particularly difficult to apply newness of life to this area of your life?

_____

_____

_____

_____

_____

_____

Take some time to envision what a life free of turmoil, worry, depression, and shame would be like. What do you see? Where are you? How do you feel? Who are you speaking to? What are you doing with your time? What does your relationship with God look like? How does it compare to the life you are living now?

_____

_____

_____

_____

Who do you have in your life who reminds you of the new life Christ has given you? Who do you know whose lives bear the fruit of newness of life? How often are you seeking counsel from them? Write down 3 pieces of wisdom you have been given over the years for walking in newness of life.

_____

_____

_____

_____

> *We were buried therefore with him by baptism into death, in order that, just as Christ was raised from the dead by glory of the Father, we too might walk in newness of life.*
>
> **—Romans 6:4**

Explain what it means to be resurrected with Christ. What are the spiritual implications of this? Why do you think we often live as if we are still dead?

_____

_____

_____

_____

What kind of growth have you noticed since becoming a follower of Christ? In what ways does your life feel new? What areas of your life need to be pruned so that you may bear the best fruit God has for you?

_____

_____

_____

_____

YOU ARE RECONCILED

As you read Day 46: "You Are Reconciled" in *Your True Reflection*, reflect on, and respond to the text by answering the following questions.

What changes have occurred in your life since being reconciled to God? Do you ever struggle with reconciling your sin with the grace we have been given because of the perfection of Jesus? Why or why not?

_____

_____

_____

_____

_____

_____

_____

Do you ever try to eliminate your sin through your works? Do you ever feel like you have to earn God's love and acceptance? What are some ways that you strive for His love?

_____

_____

_____

_____

_____

_____

Now that you have been fully reconciled to God, what kind of outcomes can you now expect in your life?

_____

_____

_____

_____

_____

How does your reconciliation to God already make you more like Jesus?

_____

_____

_____

_____

_____

_____

> *For in him all the fullness of God was pleased to dwell, and*
> *through him to reconcile to himself all things, whether on earth*
> *or in heaven, making peace by the blood of his cross.*
> —Colossians 1:19-20

What does it mean to be reconciled to God? Why does reconciliation to God bring peace? In what ways does the peace made by Christ's blood on the cross bring transformation in your life?

_____

_____

_____

_____

_____

_____

_____

Where is the evidence in your life that you have been reconciled to Him? Other than His very life, what did Jesus have to give away in order to give you everything?

_____

_____

_____

_____

_____

_____

_____

_____

YOU ARE REDEEMED

As you read Day 47: "You Are Redeemed" in *Your True Reflection*, reflect on, and respond to the text by answering the following questions.

How does the concept of being fully redeemed by Jesus' sacrifice change your perceptions of your hardships, traumas, and setbacks?

_____

_____

_____

_____

How would you explain the concept of being redeemed to someone unfamiliar with it? Have you ever done this before? How did it go? Do you feel like you have a better grasp on its meaning now than you did then?

_____

_____

_____

_____

Can you recall a moment in your life when the truth of your redemption became especially real or significant to you? What triggered this realization?

_____

_____

_____

_____

What barriers or misconceptions about redemption do you think might prevent you or others from fully accepting the reality of redemption through Jesus?

_____

_____

_____

_____

Do you know anyone who struggles with accepting the truth about their redemption, or have you known someone in the past? Why do you think this is? Can you relate to that person? In what ways?

_____

_____

_____

_____

> *In him we have redemption through his blood, the forgiveness of our trespasses, according to the riches of his grace, which he lavished upon us, in all wisdom and insight.*
>
> **—Ephesians 1:7-8**

In what ways have you experienced the richness of God's grace in your life? List a few examples and talk through how these were demonstrations of God's grace.

_____

_____

_____

_____

_____

_____

_____

Think about the word "lavished" in the context of our redemption. Why is this word so powerful in this verse? In what ways would the meaning or impact change if that phrase instead said, "which he gave us"?

_____

_____

_____

_____

_____

_____

_____

_____

YOU ARE RESTORED

As you read Day 48: "You Are Restored" in *Your True Reflection*, reflect on, and respond to the text by answering the following questions.

Have you ever identified with the blind children described in this devotional? Have you ever experienced a moment where your eyes were suddenly opened to something you didn't know was true? What did you see before? What did you see after?

_____

_____

_____

_____

_____

_____

What kind of lies are you believing about yourself? What kind of truths do you think God wants to reveal to you?

_____

_____

_____

_____

_____

_____

What part of you feels especially broken? If you could ask God to restore one thing in your life, what would it be? Be honest with yourself—do you believe He is willing and able to do it? Why or why not?

_____

_____

_____

_____

_____

_____

What aspects of yourself bind you to the prison of unworthiness? Write them down. How could you combat those perspectives with the truth that is the Word of God? Jot some Scriptures down that counter these .

_____

_____

_____

_____

Where do you feel you are needing the Spirit's strength in your life? How convinced are you that you have permanent, 24/7 access to this strength?

_____

_____

_____

_____

And after you have suffered a little while, the God of all grace, who has called you to his eternal glory in Christ, will himself restore, confirm, strengthen, and establish you.

—1 Peter 5:10

In your own life, how has God restored, confirmed, strengthened, and established you? Refer to the Greek definitions of each term for guidance.

_____

_____

_____

_____

_____

In what ways has suffering shaped your spiritual journey? In what ways has your growth along your spiritual journey shaped your experience of suffering?

_____

_____

_____

_____

YOU HAVE REWARDS IN HEAVEN THAT AWAIT YOU

As you read Day 49 "You Have Rewards in Heaven that Await You" in *Your True Reflection*, reflect on, and respond to the text by answering the following questions.

How does the concept of your rewards in heaven shape your understanding of the value and purpose of your efforts here on earth?

_____

_____

_____

_____

In what ways do you ensure that the foundations you're laying in your life align with God's purposes and values?

_____

_____

_____

_____

Can you think of any sacrifices or efforts you've made for God's kingdom that you trust have eternal significance? Give some examples.

_____

_____

_____

_____

Practically, what does it look like to build a foundation with eternity in mind?

_____

_____

_____

_____

_____

How does the promise of rewards in heaven mitigate the sting of the trials we face right now? What are you facing right now that you can leverage to reap eternal rewards?

_____

_____

_____

_____

_____

What did you learn about the two judgments that you didn't know before? Are there any parts that surprised you? Do you find encouragement in them?

_____

_____

_____

_____

> *And without faith it is impossible to please Him, for the one who comes to God must believe that He exists, and that He proves to be One who rewards those who seek Him.*
>
> **—Hebrews 11:6 (NASB)**

Based on this Scripture, what do you think God is most concerned with for the believer as it relates to receiving heavenly rewards?

_____

_____

_____

_____

_____

How do you acknowledge God's existence in your day-to-day life? How do you seek Him? What kind of rewards do you think await you as an active seeker of God?

_____

_____

_____

_____

_____

_____

YOU ARE RICH IN INHERITANCE

**As you read Day 50: "You Are Rich in Inheritance" in *Your True Reflection*,
reflect on, and respond to the text by answering the following questions.**

How does knowing you are rich in God's inheritance impact your perspective on
material wealth? In what ways have you placed your worth in earthly possessions?
Why is spiritual and eternal wealth more fulfilling?

_____

_____

_____

_____

_____

_____

_____

Review the bullet-pointed list of the benefits found in gifting things to others that
are important to them. Choose one of them and think about what about that benefit
brought you fulfillment and joy. Compare the joy you felt with the joy God feels about
sharing His inheritance with you.

_____

_____

_____

_____

_____

_____

_____

The devotional makes a profound statement: we are His purpose. What does that
mean to you?

_____

_____

_____

_____

How can you remain humble and abiding in Him when we are blessed with material wealth, keeping our eternal inheritance in mind? Do you know anyone who places greater value in their eternal inheritance than their material wealth, even if that wealth is quite large?

_____

_____

_____

_____

_____

_____

_____

_____

_____

Why is our eternal inheritance directly attached to our service to the Lord? How does our service on this earth impact our inheritance?

_____

_____

_____

_____

_____

_____

_____

_____

_____

_____

> *In him we have obtained an inheritance, having been predestined according to the purpose of him who works all things according to the counsel of his will, so that we who were the first to hope in Christ might be to the praise of his glory.*
>
> *—Ephesians 1:11-12*

YOU ARE RIGHTEOUS

As you read Day 51: "You Are Righteous" in *Your True Reflection*, reflect on, and respond to the text by answering the following questions.

How would you define righteousness? How is it different or similar to holiness?

_____

_____

_____

_____

_____

_____

Now that Christ has finished the work for you on the cross, what can you say about the discrepancy between your unrighteous behavior and the righteous child of God that Jesus has judged you to be?

_____

_____

_____

_____

_____

_____

How does your identity as a righteous child of God free you from condemnation for mistakes and sin?

_____

_____

_____

_____

_____

_____

What kind of obstacles do you face that make you feel unworthy and unrighteous? How could you use those obstacles to your advantage to write your identity as righteous before Him on your heart?

_____

_____

_____

_____

Think about a past experience when someone questioned your worthiness or spoke discouragement and condemnation over your life. If you were to face them today, what would you say to them?

_____

_____

_____

_____

> *For our sake he made him to be sin who knew no sin, so that in him we might become the righteousness of God.*
>
> —2 Corinthians 5:21

What does it mean that Jesus was "made" sin? How well do you understand that He gave His righteousness to us, sharing it freely when we didn't deserve it? What does Jesus' sacrifice to become sin for you say about how He feels about you?

_____

_____

_____

_____

Imagine you have never sinned a single day in your life. Now imagine dying a brutal death for those who were consumed by sin, including those who persecuted you. What reason would you have for making such a sacrifice? How does this compare with the reason why Jesus laid His life down for us?

_____

_____

_____

_____

_____

YOU ARE A ROYAL PRIESTHOOD

As you read Day 52: "You Are a Royal Priesthood" in *Your True Reflection*, reflect on, and respond to the text by answering the following questions.

How do you make sense of being royal (under kingship) and a priesthood (of service to others for the King)?

_____

_____

_____

_____

What could you ask God about your identity as a royal priesthood? If you could ask Him any question, what would it be? How do you think He would answer?

_____

_____

_____

_____

_____

As the priesthood of the New Covenant, how can you use prayer as an act of worship on behalf of others? What kind of power do intercessory prayer and self-sacrifice have for the edification and freeing of the captives? Have you ever experienced or witnessed this kind of power?

_____

_____

_____

_____

What does your position as a royal priesthood mean for your access to God? Do you feel like you take full advantage of this access? How could you maximize this advantage?

_____

_____

When you proclaim the goodness of God to others, how is this a visible expression of the nature and heart of God? What kind of impact do you think you, as a representative of the Almighty God, have on others who are longing for Christ?

_____

_____

_____

_____

_____

But you are a chosen race, a royal priesthood, a holy nation, a people for his own possession, that you may proclaim the excellencies of him who called you out of darkness into his marvelous light.

—1 Peter 2:9

How would you describe what it looks like and feels like to be royalty? Now insert yourself in the position of a royal heir and imagine coming into Jesus's court. What do you see? How do you feel? Describe the vision.

_____

_____

_____

_____

_____

Can you think of a time when you were lost in the darkness? What kind of experiences did you have? What kind of thoughts appeared about yourself and your future? How does that change knowing that you have been cordially invited by the King Himself into His throne room?

_____

_____

_____

_____

_____

YOU ARE A SAINT

**As you read Day 53: "You Are a Saint" in *Your True Reflection*, reflect
on, and respond to the text by answering the following questions.**

God considers you to be His saint. How does that change your perspective about
yourself? What exactly does it mean to be God's saint?

_____

_____

_____

_____

What does God require of you to become His saint? What makes you His saint?

_____

_____

_____

_____

What responsibilities come with being considered a saint? How does God equip you
to live as a saint? Do you anticipate that God will come alongside you in your efforts
to love like a saint?

_____

_____

_____

_____

What can you do to embrace your new position as a saint for God? Do you embrace
it now? Can you think of an example in your life when you have helped someone
else thrive?

_____

_____

_____

_____

We don't always feel like saints. We are broken just like everyone else. But how do you think others, particularly those who don't know Jesus, see you? If you knew that you played an important role in changing someone's life, how would that impact what you see when you look in the mirror?

He who searches the hearts knows what is the mind of the Spirit, because the Spirit intercedes for the saints according to the will of God.

—Romans 8:27

What does it feel like to know that God searches your heart? Why does He do that? What do you think God has found? How does God see your heart differently than you see your own?

Do you ever feel exhausted in your prayer life, as if you have nothing else to say, unsure of what to ask God? How does His intercession for your unspoken prayers relieve pressure from your heart to pray perfectly?

YOU ARE THE SALT OF THE EARTH

As you read Day 54: "You Are the Salt of the Earth" in *Your True Reflection*, reflect on, and respond to the text by answering the following questions.

What does it mean to you to be the "salt of the earth" practically? Can you think of a time when you have been salt to the world and others? Can you think of a time when you lost your saltiness? What happened and how did it impact you or others?

_____

_____

_____

_____

_____

_____

_____

How do you maintain your "saltiness" in a world that opposes Christian values?

_____

_____

_____

_____

_____

Does being the salt of the earth align with how you see yourself? What does being salt require of you to stand out or be different than others?

_____

_____

_____

_____

_____

In what ways have you experienced challenges or opposition in being salt? Why did you think that is? How did you respond? How were you able to keep moving forward and preserve your salti-ness?

_____

_____

_____

_____

_____

What does it take to maintain your saltiness? What would it do for your self-image if you could preserve your saltiness?

_____

_____

_____

_____

_____

> *"You are the salt of the earth, but if salt has lost its taste, how shall its saltiness be restored? It is no longer good for anything except to be thrown out and trampled under people's feet."*
> —Matthew 5:13

How does this Scripture make you feel? What kind of questions come up for you?

_____

_____

_____

_____

_____

Why is it so important to pursue a life of saltiness in a broken world? How does the grace afforded to us by Jesus play a role in our fight to become salt?

_____

_____

_____

_____

_____

YOU ARE SEALED THROUGH SALVATION

**As you read Day 55: "You Are Sealed Through Salvation"
in *Your True Reflection*, reflect on, and respond to the
text by answering the following questions.**

What does it mean to you personally to be secured by God?

_____

_____

_____

_____

_____

_____

_____

How does the assurance of salvation impact your views on eternity? How does it
enable you to keep your eyes on things eternal, rather than the temporal things of this
world? How does this alter your perspective of your identity in Him?

_____

_____

_____

_____

_____

_____

_____

If you are sealed in Christ with the guarantee of His inheritance, how does that help
you fulfill your mission here on earth? How does it change the way you experience the
mundane things of life?

_____

_____

_____

_____

_____

_____

_____

_____

_____

God chose you to receive all that He has because of the seal of salvation through Christ Jesus. What does this say about how important you are for the body of Christ to operate properly?

_____

_____

_____

_____

_____

_____

_____

How is your life evidence that God has more for you and needs more from you? How is God using the promise of your salvation now to set you apart as a valuable asset to the Kingdom?

_____

_____

_____

_____

_____

_____

_____

> *In him you also, when you heard the word of truth, the gospel of your salvation, and believed in him, were sealed with the promised Holy Spirit, who is the guarantee of our inheritance until we acquire possession of it, to the praise of his glory.*
>
> —Ephesians 1:13-14

YOU SHARE IN CHRIST'S SUFFERING

As you read Day 56: "You Share in Christ's Suffering" in *Your True Reflection*, reflect on, and respond to the text by answering the following questions.

Sometimes, knowing that we now share in Christ's suffering can be a hard pill to swallow. How can you find encouragement in this? Why can we consider this an honor and privilege?

_____

_____

_____

_____

Do you ever feel that our suffering for Christ is a burden? In what ways do you find comfort in knowing that Christ also suffered?

_____

_____

_____

_____

In what ways can your sufferings bring you closer to Christ? What would this mean for your life and the lives of others that you touch?

_____

_____

_____

_____

If you never experienced any suffering, would it impact your intimacy with Christ? How so? Would it be possible to find closeness with Jesus without suffering?

_____

_____

_____

_____

How do you think Jesus feels about those who share in the suffering of Christ?

_____

_____

_____

_____

How is your suffering alongside Christ a memento of His love and care for you?

_____

_____

_____

_____

> *Beloved, do not be surprised at the fiery trial when it comes upon you to test you, as through something strange were happening to you. But rejoice insofar as you share Christ's sufferings, that you may also rejoice and be glad when his glory is revealed.*
>
> **—1 Peter 4:12-13**

We have all been blindsided by trials we didn't anticipate before. How can you better prepare your heart for such trials? How can you leverage them to share in His glory?

_____

_____

_____

_____

_____

_____

The Scripture mentions that trials will come to test you. What is your experience with spiritual tests? Explain what it did for you.

_____

_____

_____

_____

_____

_____

YOU ARE THE TEMPLE OF THE HOLY SPIRIT

As you read Day 57: "You Are the Temple of the Holy Spirit" in *Your True Reflection*, reflect on, and respond to the text by answering the following questions.

How does knowing you are a temple of the Holy Spirit influence your actions and choices? What does it mean to honor your body as the temple of the Holy Spirit?

_____

_____

_____

_____

How can you ensure that your life reflects the indwelling of the Holy Spirit?

_____

_____

_____

_____

What is it like for you to know that you are now the modern-day Most Holy Place, where God is present at all times?

_____

_____

_____

_____

In what ways do you experience the Holy Spirit's presence in your life? Does it ever feel like He is nowhere to be found? Why do you think that is and what can you do to resist that feeling?

_____

_____

_____

_____

_____

What practices help you to stay aligned with the Holy Spirit's guidance and presence? When do you feel the most separated from Him? Why?

_____

_____

_____

_____

_____

> *Therefore go out from their midst, and be separate from them, says the Lord, and touch no unclean thing; then I will welcome you, and I will be a father to you, and you shall be sons and daughters to me, says the Lord Almighty."*
>
> —2 Corinthians 6:17-18

What agreement has the temple of God with idols?

_____

_____

_____

_____

What do you think Paul means when he asks "what agreement has the temple of God with idols"? How do idols squander the joy of life in the Spirit that has been deposited within you?

_____

_____

_____

_____

What is God's heart behind his command to separate from idols? What is He trying to accomplish? What is He hoping to free you from by urging you to remove any idols that have taken up residence in your heart?

_____

_____

_____

_____

YOU ARE WASHED

As you read Day 58: "You Are Washed" in *Your True Reflection*, reflect on, and respond to the text by answering the following questions.

How does knowing you are washed by the blood of Jesus impact your identity? What exactly does being washed mean?

_____

_____

_____

_____

Do you ever remain tethered to your old self? In what ways does your old self hold you captive?

_____

_____

_____

_____

If you could live your life with perfect knowledge that the blood of Jesus has made you clean for all eternity, what would your life look like? What kind of effect would that have on your life and relationships?

_____

_____

_____

_____

What does the phrase "His mercies are new every morning" mean to you? Do you allow your emotions to dictate the course of your day and the weight of the shame of your past? How so?

_____

_____

_____

_____

God sent the most precious treasure—His son, Jesus Christ—to be a living sacrifice for your sins. How does Jesus's bloodshed secure your confidence that He has made you forever clean?

_____

_____

_____

_____

_____

> *"After that, he poured water into a basin and began to wash his disciples' feet, drying them with the towel that was wrapped around him. He came to Simon Peter, who said to him, 'Lord, are you going to wash my feet?' Jesus replied, 'You do not realize now what I am doing, but later you will understand.' 'No,' said Peter, 'you shall never wash my feet.' Jesus answered, 'Unless I wash you, you have no part with me.' 'Then, Lord,' Simon Peter replied, 'not just my feet but my hands and my head as well!'"*
>
> —John 13:5-9 (NIV)

Why do you think Jesus washed the feet of His disciples? What was He trying to teach them?

_____

_____

_____

_____

_____

What does Peter's response say about how we sometimes respond to the finality of Jesus' sacrifice? How does living a life defeated and ashamed deny the work that Jesus did for us?

_____

_____

_____

_____

_____

_____

YOU HAVE WISDOM AND REVELATION

**As you read Day 59: "You Have Wisdom and Revelation"
in *Your True Reflection*, reflect on, and respond to the
text by answering the following questions.**

How do you discern the difference between worldly wisdom and God's wisdom in daily situations? In what ways is this a challenge for you? Conversely, in what ways has it become easier for you as you have matured in your walk with the Lord? Think of an example for each.

_____

_____

_____

_____

What does it mean to you to have the mind of Christ? What kind of mind did Christ have? What were His thoughts, and in what ways did He walk with perfect wisdom?

_____

_____

_____

_____

Can you think of a time when you received divine revelation from God about something? Were you actively searching for that revelation or was it unexpected? How did it change you?

_____

_____

_____

_____

How do you respond when God's wisdom seems counterintuitive to human understanding?

_____

_____

_____

In what ways are you resistant to allowing God to shape you and form you to conform to His will? Are you willing to let go of your will to make room for His wisdom as He leads you where He wants you?

_____

_____

_____

_____

_____

> *Now to Him who is able to establish you according to my gospel and the preaching of Jesus Christ, according to the revelation of the mystery which has been kept secret for long ages past.*
>
> **—Romans 16:25 (NASB)**

What does it mean to be established in the gospel? What does this have to do with the wisdom and divine revelation God has given you through Jesus Christ?

_____

_____

_____

_____

_____

_____

What kind of things do you think God is waiting to reveal to you as you go deeper in your pursuit of His presence and Word?

_____

_____

_____

_____

_____

_____

YOU ARE HIS WORKMANSHIP

As you read Day 60: "You Are His Workmanship" in *Your True Reflection*, reflect on, and respond to the text by answering the following questions.

When you think about being God's workmanship, what comes to mind? What does that really mean to you?

_____

_____

_____

_____

In what ways can you see God's craftmanship in your abilities and talents?

_____

_____

_____

_____

Do you ever feel like you are an accident? How can you begin to think differently?

_____

_____

_____

_____

How do you navigate comparison to others, keeping in mind that you are uniquely crafted by God? What are the stories you tell yourself when it seems like your peers seem to have it easier than you, more to offer than you, or are living the life you want to live?

_____

_____

_____

_____

_____

What aspects of your life clearly reflect that you are intricately designed by God? Have your friends, family, co-workers, or pastor ever shared the areas that you seem to excel in? Did you see any patterns or consistency?

_____

_____

_____

_____

_____

What beautiful thing do you think God is wanting to produce in your life? How are you partnering with Him to accomplish that?

_____

_____

_____

_____

_____

> *For we are his workmanship, created in Christ Jesus for good works, which God prepared beforehand, that we should walk in them.*
>
> **—Ephesians 2:10**

If God prepared you and everything about you and in you before you were even created, what does this say about the special interest He has in you?

_____

_____

_____

_____

_____

What kind of good works do you feel that God is calling you to? What do you think He made you for?

_____

_____

_____

_____

_____